LIFE
IN A
GLASS BOX

Emily L. Emery

authorHOUSE

AuthorHouse™
1663 Liberty Drive
Bloomington, IN 47403
www.authorhouse.com
Phone: 833-262-8899

Published by AuthorHouse 08/17/2023

ISBN: 979-8-8230-1349-9 (sc)
ISBN: 979-8-8230-1348-2 (e)

LIFE IN A GLASS BOX

Imagine living life in a glass box. Always looking out. Always separate from everything that passes. Sometimes people reach out and try and grab you. Pull you closer to everything that happens, but eventually they give up in frustration because you never grab their hand. They don't see the glass box that encases you. They don't know how bad you wanted to. It seems the only thing that the glass box manages to do for the outside looking in, is give off an aloofness. A distance. A manner of extreme superiority. And everyone on the outside looks in and screams "snob!"

Imagine life on the inside. You try to engage in life on the outside. But everything you say and everything you do through glass just comes out warped. Empathy is hard to indulge in. The glass box is full of all your problems and though small, sometimes is more than you can hold. People on the outside look in, and scream "Narcissist!" but inside you're full of self-loathing. You're tired of your own company. Sometimes you try to let people in, but as soon as they approach, you shut back up again. The glass box has made you fragile. Sticks and stones don't hurt if thrown from the outside, but inside, imagine what they'd do. You don't have the strength to heal yourself of someone hurts you. It all just goes to just surviving. Life in a glass box wasn't your choosing, and though it's not something that could ever happen it's something that every day you try and undo.

SECRETS

Red roses are for love
Red and white, unity.
White is for a secret,
That I will keep to me.
The secret that I will not share,
I wish I could forget,
But if I were to tell you…
Can you keep a secret?

UNFINISHED DREAMS

They call to me, my unfinished dreams.
Stretching as far as I see.
They show me all I can be,
But right now, I'm still only me.

The fantasy, I created about goals,
Show me success, while still leaving holes.
It contrasts to how the world is.
It blocks out the struggles and risks.

So, I stand frozen, in undecidedness.
I know what I want, what I hope, what I wish.
Yet how do I get there to attain what moves me.
How do I finish my unfinished dreams?

SNAPSHOTS

Snapshots of old memories playing in your mind.

Taken from a moment now forever frozen in time.

The smiling faces haunt you because you know that now they're gone.

You wish that you could sooth them, and prepare them for what's to come.

You wish that you could stop them from letting the moment slide.

Because what's gone is gone forever, no matter how hard you might try.

All that's left is old snapshots, but even those have begun to fade.

All you hold now is the memory, of a different time a different place.

A different person altogether, never to be seen or heard again,

Except in maybe snapshots. Smile, flash,

The end

SHE THAT IS FIRST

You may call me heartless, and heartless I may be.

But I never gave my heart away, nor had it stolen from me.

The fact is I've sold it. It was the price I paid to get ahead.

The very thing I thought would save me, was the thing that tripped me in the end.

Run the race! Is what they told me, and it's exactly what I've done.

After everything I did to get here, how is it I haven't won?

I gave my soul for an advantage. I traded trust for higher ground.

I left self-integrity a long time ago. A lot of good it does me now.

When I had finally made it, to the finish line

It was with dismay I realized I could not cross because I left myself behind.

CAN'T HOLD WATER

You can't hold water in a glass that has been cracked.

No matter how much you pour into me,

I'll never quite be full.

You can't live out your fantasies, through a book full of facts.

No matter how exciting you want me to be,

I can only always be dull.

Don't build me up into something I'm not.

Don't expect more than I can do.

Because you can't hold water in a glass that's cracked,

However badly you may want to.

DANCER

If life's a dance, I'll dance my hardest
Though no one dance with me.
I'll pour my heart and soul into it,
I'll give it all of me.
I'll try my best to reach perfection.
Though perfection I'll never reach.
Because if life's a dance, danced upon a stage,
Then a dancer I will be.

AFRAID TO FLY

See these wings they're made for flying.

When I take off, all watch me soar.

They stop to marvel at my beauty,

Reaching heights not reached before.

What they don't know is, I'm afraid of flying.

What would happen if I fall?

Still they applaud me higher, higher.

So, I obey the greater call.

I'm flying upwards and onward,
All I see before me is sky.
I am one with the heavens,
And there is no one else but I.
But all I'm thinking is what could happen,
If I'm shot down from these heights.
I must not let it happen unexpected,
So, I search for early signs.

I'm flying but I'm uneasy,
And my eyes always are on the ground.
Searching for a soft landing,
Because I'm safer on the ground.
What a joke, a freak of nature.
A waste of feathers am I.
I'm the mess up, I'm the failure,
I'm the bird afraid to fly.

EMPTY BOTTLES

You don't kill the pain,
You just give it all away.
Then I guess it is mine to bear,
Every single day.
I tried to quiet my thoughts,
And lay down for an eternal sleep.
My thoughts only grew louder,
My pain I only felt more.
I reached out and no one grabbed me.
Who do I bear this for?
I tried to bleed out my problems,
In a red river I would drown.
But my problems only became more prominent
And there was no solution to be found.
I lay down with all my problems
Empty bottles and red sheets
It is a messed-up thing that life is
And the biggest disappointment in it is me
I always thought that I'd be better
I always thought that I was good
Now I don't want to reach tomorrow
And d forget yesterday if I could
All I'm thinking of is this moment
Who I am and if I'll be
I lay down with all my choices
Empty bottles and red sheets.

PRETENDER

I built myself a castle.
I made myself the queen.
I chose a prince to come and join me,
He would be my king.
I picked the lands that we would conquer.
I spoke of the riches we would hold,
But when the veil finally lifted,
It was stories I had told.

My castle is made of paper.
I am not a queen.
My prince he never loved me.
How absurd now it all seems.
I was just pretending,
That everything was grand.
Now that I'm not pretending,
Everything looks bland.

My paper walls are tearing.
My crown it has no shine.
My prince he loves another.
Never again will he be mine.

It was a dream that I was dreaming.
It was a pretend world that I had lived.
Now my dreams have all ended,
And I'll never pretend again.

If I can't have my castle,
If I can't have my king,
If I can't live out my stories,
There's no use in my pretending.

TIME

One day at a time.

One minute after the other.

I'll get over you again.

It took time to get to where I was before.

One painful hour after hour.

It took one look from you to wipe it all away.

Brick by brick I had built a wall to distance myself from you.

Now it is gone.

I'm standing before you. You're looking at me. We are back where we were. Young, and in love and stupid.

For one second, I am lost.

For one second, I am found.

I am in a place I know well.

I'm listening to a voice I've heard often.

I feel a touch I've not even allowed myself to dream about lately.

It's all back. It's all mine. You turn away,

And it's all gone.

Painfully.

God the pain is insufferable!

I put the first brick back in its place.

I must build my wall again.

Time is all it takes.

As I go on I know the bricks just get lighter.

Pretty soon I'll have it built so tall.

But the first bricks are always the hardest.

A broken heart can't fuel my strength and right now I have none.

My heart is still bleeding.

I can still you see you walking away on the other side.

It's a fight against myself not to beg you to come back and fix me, for just one second, as I know you can.

But each time you leave me you break me further than I've ever been broke before.

It's all I can do to keep my heart beating with all the cracks of every time it's been shattered.

Pretty soon I won't be able to go on.

Painfully.

God the pain!

I wish I'd never met you!

I'd never know the pain that I feel now!

I place the second brick back in its place.

Time is all it takes.

I know this.

But good God please give me the strength!

MY KINGDOM'S END

I thought life was forever,
That happiness was free.
That all it took to build a kingdom,
Was ambition, drive, and dreams.
I thought there was a right,
And I knew there was a wrong,
And the path that leads to heaven,
Was easy to follow along.
I never dreamed the end would come so fast,
That happiness cost so much.

That all my kingdom's walls would cave in,
When life became too tough.
That black and white would mix,
Into confusing shades of grey.
And on a path that went so straight,
I could easily lose my way.
I stand among the ruin,
Of what used to be my home.
No longer sheltered by walls of fancy,
All my dreams having gone.
A merciless wind blows upon me,
Of what they dare call facts of life.
The world goes around and round.
You're born, you live, you die.
There's nothing I can do to stop that.
Nothing I can do to go back.
Nothing I can do to right my wrongs.
Nothing I can do to change my path.
Nothing I can do to save myself
From this ruin that I'm in.
This is the turning of a page.
This is my kingdoms end.

THE BOTTOM

I'm here at the bottom
I sit here in darkness
I stay by myself
Because here, I know I can

Some people will look down
Some try and save me
Some actually reach out
They try to get me to take their hand

But I'm here at the bottom
Because I crave the darkness
There's no further to fall
No hope to be found

I'm here at the bottom
And nobody pushed me
I don't need you to break me
I did it myself when I came down

So, don't try and fix me
However badly my brokenness makes you ache
I'd rather be breaking and alone
Then be with you as you watch me break

I'm just a mess up
I'm not supposed to be here
I'm just a sick joke
And it's more than I can take

I'm here at the bottom
Where no one can reach me
No one can see me
I'm a monster who needs to be alone

Don't trust me to be sane
Don't trust I can be fixed
I'd probably break you
Then you too would be gone.

SAD

I feel so sad. My sadness hurts me
I feel too sad to just be fine.
Maybe it's a different kind of sadness
Unlike the one I've lived with all my life.
Maybe it's a normal reaction to normal events.
The end of us. The loss of you.
What a relief it would be to know it ends,
If only I knew it to be true.
It's hard to imagine there's a different kind of sadness,
Then the one I've lived with everyday
The one that's there even when I'm happy.
The kind that never goes away.
Maybe this sadness is just a moment.
It's not forever. It's not for life.
No, this sadness is not forever.
It's just until I die…

WE WERE

I thought you'd meet me halfway with all my efforts.

I thought you'd take my pain away.

I thought I'd be yours and you'd be mine forever.

I thought once I had you, you would stay.

Instead you reached your arms out as if to catch me

But you changed your mind halfway through.

I dove head first without looking,

If at the bottom I'd still get you.

I fell and kept on falling,

Until finally I hit the floor.

You just looked at me with all my problems,

And shrugged and said "Here's more."

You weren't the savior I was looking for,

I wasn't the angel that you would want.

We weren't a match made in heaven

We just were until we weren't.

Let's say it didn't happen
Let's pretend it isn't so
Let's close our eyes on all this madness
Maybe all this sadness too will go
Let's pretend that we are all right
Let's make believe we're fine
Let's ignore all the questions
All we need is time
But it happened and it's horrid
The nightmare lives with you still
Close your eyes and it's before you
Consuming everything you feel
The questions keep on coming
There's nothing you could do to make it stop
All these horrors of this lifetime
Are better off forgot

PEDESTAL

They place me on a stool too high for me
And all seemed dismayed when I fall
But their satisfied smiles, and dismissal shrugs
Make me wonder if they cared at all
They all seemed so eager to see me succeed
In a way they were holding me back
Because while they applauded and built me up
They were seeking the traits that I lacked
I thought they sincerely thought I was great
And while they looked, I played the fool
One by one now they're turning their backs
I've fallen off my pedestal.

MY TIME

Was the time I spent, spent wisely?

I really can't remember.

Were the memories I made,

Built to last forever?

Did I take the time to learn,

From my trials, and troubles, and strife?

Did I take the time to enrich,

And better my life?

I search my mind for answers,

But there are no answers that I can find

What did I really do,

That used up all my time?

I spent my time sparingly
And as I reach for more it's gone
Was that really a lifetime?
It didn't feel like very long.
It felt like forever was facing me,
And now suddenly I'm facing the end.
But what steps did I take to get here?
When did I even begin?
I search my mind for answers

But there are no answers I can find.
What did I really do,
That used up all my time?

I was planning to better my future,
But I guess my future came too fast.
When did what was my present,
Now become my past?
I guess even if you never move forward
Time moves forward still,
And your time on earth gets spent regardless
Even in ways against your will
I search my mind for answers,
Until at last I find,
If I could do it over,
I'd find ways that I'd remember
What I did with all my time.

DARKNESS

You can make believe you're happy
You can smile wide
When you're dancing in the sunlight
There's no place your troubles hide
But when the sun starts to sink down
And the shadows start to come
It's time to face your demons
And leave off soaking in the sun

Did you really think you were happy?

How could you be when you knew this would come?

Darkness always follows daylight

Clouds always mask the sun

Happiness is just a moment

Blink once and it's gone

Daylight gives way to twilight

And the night goes on and on

Darkness overcomes you

It covers you like an unwanted coat

The terror overtakes you

Like a hand that grasps your throat

And all night you feel you're sinking

The more you try, the faster the sinking goes

Pretty soon you're at the bottom

With all your demons, and problems, and woes

And maybe you scream

But no one can hear you

And if they did

There's nothing they'd do

The darkness is not their problem

The darkness belongs to you

Pretty soon you embrace it

Because now it's all you know

And just as that starts to happen

The darkness starts to go

Now you're standing in the dew dipped morning

Pretty soon you'll see the sun

But even standing in the daylight

All your happiness is gone

So, go ahead, pretend you're happy

Dance and smile like a well- trained act

You may be standing in the sunshine

But we all know

The darkness always comes back

BEST OF ME

I gave you the very best of me,
In return you walked away
I'm sorry my best was not enough
I'm sorry you couldn't stay
You left, but you didn't break me
I'm sad, but I'm not through
Because now I have the best of me,
It's no longer being wasted on you.

MIRAGE

I was in a desert chasing a mirage

But of course, when I reached it, it was gone.

You see, it never really existed,

It just led me on.

Now I sit here in the desert,

Waiting for what doesn't exist to return to me.

But I'll never get what wasn't there

So in a way, I'll never be free

I thirst I starve I slowly die

But I never ask if I should just leave?

I wait, I cry, I scream, I beg,

In my own way I grieve.

For a mirage. For an illusion,

For what I thought It was.

But it was nothing, and I gave it everything,

To be left with nothing but dust.

WHAT GOES AROUND

What goes around comes back around,
And round and round it goes.
I wish that I could catch it,
Where's it stop? No one knows.
What goes around comes back around,
And round and round it swings,
But if what goes around comes back around,
Why hasn't it come back round to me?
I've been standing still waiting
Waiting to make things right
But what goes around never comes back around,
To those that keep mistakes in sight.
Life's a cruel game we've been playing
And it's dealt some heavy blows.
Most of which were come backs,
Strike for strike, throw for throw
It was this one fact that I was counting
Glove in hand, I wait to make my catch
But what goes around doesn't come back around
In this game, there's no second chance,

GOODBYE

How can I explain your absence?
It's a void, a missing piece, a conversation that can't be had.
It's lonely, and overwhelming,
It's isolating and sad
How can I explain my feelings?
I feel somehow set free
I feel weightless, I feel able
I feel like once again, I am me.
I'm sad for having lost you,
But I don't feel bad for letting go
You see, I couldn't save you,
And it took me until now to know
I'm not saying I was always unhappy
I'm not saying it was always bad
You gave me some of the best times,
Some of the best memories I had.
I'm saying that while I valued and viewed these memories
With the highest regard
To you they became nothing
And to me that will always be hard
To understand how my everyhting, became nothing to you
How little you thought of all the sacrifices I made
So how can I explain your absence?

It was the high price I paid
For my happiness, for my independence
For all of my success
I deserve these in abundance,
And I no longer will settle for less
So I hope somehow you will be happy,
It was you that chose this life
And I can no longer go with you
So for me, this is goodbye...

Printed in the United States
by Baker & Taylor Publisher Services